To

_____

From

_____

Date

_____

50 Daily Devotions

for Kids only

Obedience

50 Daily Devotions

for Kids only

Obedience

A Message to Parents

Congratulations on picking up this book! It proves that you're a thoughtful parent who is interested in both the spiritual and intellectual development of your child.

This text, which is intended to be read by Christian parents to their young children, contains 50 brief chapters. Each chapter examines a different aspect of an important Biblical theme: obedience.

For the next 50 days, try this experiment: read one chapter each night to your child, and then spend a few more moments talking about the chapter's meaning. By doing so, you will have had 50 different opportunities to share God's wisdom with your son or daughter, and that's a very good thing.

If you have been touched by God's love and His grace, then you know the joy that He has brought into your own life. Now it's your turn to share His message with the boy or girl whom He has entrusted to your care. Happy reading! And may God richly bless you and your family now and forever.

Day 1

God Has Rules

We can be sure that we know God
if we obey his commands.

1 John 2:3 NCV

God has rules, and He wants you to obey them. He wants you to be fair, honest, and kind. He wants you to behave yourself, and He wants you to respect your parents. God has other rules, too, and you'll find them in a very special book: the Bible.

With a little help from your parents, you can figure out God's rules. And then, it's up to you to live by them. When you do, everybody will be pleased—you'll be pleased, your parents will be pleased . . . and God will be pleased, too.

Nobody is good by accident.

C. H. Spurgeon

A Parent's Tip!

Teaching Them Obedience: Your children will learn about life from many sources; the most important source should be you. But remember that the lectures you give are never as important as the ones you live.

A Kid's Tip!

Obeying God? Yes! What about all those rules you learn about in the Bible? Well, those aren't just any old rules—they're God's rules. And you should behave—and obey—accordingly.

Today's Prayer

Dear Lord, I trust You, and I know that
Your rules are good for me.
I will do my best to obey You,
even when it's hard.
Amen

Day 2

Your Family Has Rules

You must choose for yourselves today
whom you will serve . . . as for me and my family,
we will serve the Lord.

Joshua 24:15 NCV

Your family has rules . . . rules that you're not supposed to break.

If you're old enough to know right from wrong, then you're old enough to do something about it. In other words, you should always try to obey your family's rules.

How can you tell "the right thing" from "the wrong thing"? By listening carefully to your parents, that's how. So here's what you should do: First, slow down long enough to listen to your parents. Then, do the things that you know your parents want you to do.

Face facts: your family has rules . . . and it's better for everybody when you obey them.

The child that never learns to obey
his parents in the home will not obey God
or man out of the home.

Susanna Wesley

A Parent's Tip!

Wise parents know what to overlook. Expect your child to be well behaved, but don't expect your child to be perfect.

A Kid's Tip!

Since you love your family . . . show it by behaving yourself and obeying your family's rules!

Today's Prayer

Dear Lord, You have given me a family
that cares for me and loves me.
Thank You. Let me love everybody in my
family, even when they're not perfect.
And let me always be thankful that
my family loves me even when
I'm not perfect.
Amen

Day 3

It's in the Bible

Your word is like a lamp for my feet
and a light for my way.

Psalm 119:105 ICB

What book contains everything that God has to say about obedience? The Bible, of course. If you read the Bible every day, you'll soon be convinced that obedience is very important to God. And, since obedience is important to God, it should be important to you, too.

The Bible is the most important book you'll ever own. It's God's Holy Word. Read it every day, and follow its instructions. If you do, you'll be a more obedient person . . . and you'll be safe now and forever.

The Bible is the treasure map that leads us
to God's highest treasures.

Max Lucado

A Parent's Tip!

How can you teach your children the importance of
God's Holy Word? By example. When teaching your
child about the Bible, words are fine—but actually
living the Bible is far better.

A Kid's Tip!

Do you take care of your Bible? Hopefully so! After
all, it's the most important book you'll ever own!

Today's Prayer

Dear Lord, the Bible is Your gift to me.
Let me use, let me trust it, and let me
obey it, today and every day.
Amen

Day 4

Obey and Be Happy

But the truly happy person is the one who carefully
studies God's perfect law that makes people free.
He continues to study it. He listens to
God's teaching and does not forget what he heard.
Then he obeys what God's teaching says.
When he does this, it makes him happy.

James 1:25 ICB

Do you want to be happy? Then you should learn to obey your parents and your teachers. And, of course, you should also learn to obey God. When you do, you'll discover that happiness goes hand-in-hand with good behavior.

The happiest people do not misbehave; the happiest people are not cruel or greedy. The happiest people don't disobey their parents, their teachers, or their Father in heaven. The happiest people are those who obey the rules . . .

And it's up to you to make sure that you're one of those happy people.

Happiness is obedience,
and obedience is happiness.

C. H. Spurgeon

A Parent's Tip!

Your positive responses to their positive behavior:
When your child does something good, applaud
loudly. When you do, you'll make two people happy.

A Kid's Tip!

Good behavior leads to a happy life. And bad
behavior doesn't.

Today's Prayer

Dear Heavenly Father, when I obey,
I'm a much happier person. Help me learn
the importance of obeying my parents
and the importance of obeying You.
Amen

Day 5

Think About It First

So prepare your minds for service and have
self-control. All your hope should be for
the gift of grace that will be yours when
Jesus Christ is shown to you.

1 Peter 1:13 NCV

Maybe you've heard this old saying: "Look before you leap." What does that saying mean? It means that you should stop and think before you do something. Otherwise, you might be sorry you did it.

Learning how to control yourself is an important part of growing up. The more you learn about self-control, the better. Self-control will help you at home, at school, and at church. That's why parents and teachers are happy to talk about the rewards of good self-control. And that's why you should be excited about learning how important it is to look before you leap . . . not after!

Plan ahead—it wasn't raining when
Noah built the ark.

Anonymous

A Parent's Tip!

Be patient with your child's impatience: children are supposed to be more impulsive than adults; after all, they're still kids. So be understanding of your child's limitations and understanding of his or her imperfections.

A Kid's Tip!

Controlling yourself by slowing yourself down: Sometimes, the best way to control yourself is to slow yourself down. Then, you can think about the things you're about to do before you do them.

Today's Prayer

Dear Lord, the Bible teaches me that it's good to be able to control myself. Today, I will slow myself down and think about things before I do things.
Amen

Day 6

Obeying Your Parents

Children, obey your parents in all things:
for this is well-pleasing unto the Lord.

Colossians 3:20 KJV

When your parents ask you to do something, do you usually obey them or do you usually ignore them? When your parents try to get your attention, do you listen or not? When your parents make rules, do you obey those rules or do you break them? Hopefully, you've learned to listen to your parents and to obey.

In order to be an obedient person, you must first learn how to control yourself—otherwise, you won't be able to behave yourself even if you want to. Controlling yourself means that you must slow down long enough to listen to your parents, and then you must be willing to do something about the things your parents tell you to do.

When you learn the importance of obedience, you'll soon discover that good things happen when you behave yourself. And the sooner you learn to listen and to obey, the sooner those good things will start happening . . . to you!

He intended families to be the safe haven
where children are born and raised, a place where
the tender shoots are nurtured until their roots
grow strong and deep.

Carol Kuykendall

A Parent's Tip!

Have a Few Important Rules . . . and enforce them.

A Kid's Tip!

When you obey your parents . . . you're pleasing
God, you're pleasing your parents, and you're doing
yourself a BIG favor.

Today's Prayer

Dear Lord, when I obey Your rules,
good things happen. One of Your rules is
pretty simple: to obey my parents.
So here's what I'm asking for, Lord:
Help me listen to my parents . . .
and help me obey them.
Amen

Choices Have Consequences

Do not be fooled: You cannot cheat God.
People harvest only what they plant.

Galatians 6:7-8 NCV

There's really no way to get around it: choices matter. If you make good choices, good things will usually happen to you. And if you make bad choices, bad things will usually happen.

The next time you have an important choice to make, ask yourself this: "Am I doing what God wants me to do?" If you can answer that question with a great big "YES," then go ahead. But if you're not sure if the choice you are about to make is right, slow down. Why? Because choices matter . . . a lot!

It is easy to dodge our responsibilities,
but we cannot dodge the consequences
of dodging our responsibilities.

Josiah Stamp

A Parent's Tip!

Logical Consequences! The world won't protect
your child from the consequences of misbehavior,
and neither should you. As a parent, your job is to
ensure that the consequences of your child's actions
are logical, measured, appropriate, and thoroughly
understood by your youngster.

A Kid's Tip!

Think ahead: Before you do something, ask yourself
this question: "Will I be ashamed if my parents find
out?" If the answer to that question is "Yes," don't
do it!

Today's Prayer

Dear Lord, when I play by Your rules,
You bless my life. But, when I disobey
Your rules, I suffer the consequences.
Help me obey You and my parents . . .
starting right now!
Amen

Day 8

Listen to Your Conscience

They show that in their hearts they know
what is right and wrong.

Romans 2:15 ICB

*G*od gave you something called a conscience: some people describe it as a little voice, but really, it's a feeling—it's a feeling that tells you whether something is right or wrong. Your conscience will usually tell you what to do and when to do it. Pay attention to that feeling, and trust it.

If you slow down and listen to your conscience, you'll usually stay out of trouble. And if you listen to your conscience, it won't be so hard to control your own behavior. Why? Because most of the time, your conscience already knows right from wrong. So don't be in such a hurry to do things. Instead of "jumping right in," listen to your conscience. In the end, you'll be very glad you did.

Your conscience is your alarm system.
It's your protection.

Charles Stanley

A Parent's Tip!

Sometimes, the little voice that we hear in our heads can be the echoes of our own parents' voices . . . and now that we're parents ourselves, we're the ones whose words will echo down through the hearts and minds of future generations. It's a big responsibility, but with God's help, we'll be up to the challenge.

A Kid's Tip!

If you're not sure what to do . . . trust your conscience. It's almost always right!

Today's Prayer

Dear Lord, You have given me
a conscience that tells me what is right
and what is wrong. I will listen to that
quiet voice so I can do the right thing
today and every day.
Amen

Day 9

Don't Whine!

Your attitude should be the same that
Christ Jesus had.

Philippians 2:5 NLT

Do you like to listen to other children whine? No way! And since you don't like to hear other kids whining, then you certainly shouldn't whine, either.

Sometimes, kids think that whining is a good way to get the things they want . . . but it's not! So if your parents or your teacher ask you to do something, don't complain about it. And if there's something you want, don't whine and complain until you get it.

Remember: whining won't make you happy . . . and it won't make anybody else happy, either.

Shine—don't whine.

Anonymous

A Parent's Tip!

Count your blessings . . . and keep counting. Whining can be contagious, so make sure that your home is, to the greatest extent possible, a whine-free zone. How can you do this? A good way to start is by counting your blessings, not your problems.

A Kid's Tip!

Two special words: Thank you! Your parents and your teachers will never become tired of hearing those two little words. Say them often.

Today's Prayer

Dear Lord, I'm really thankful for all
the good things I have. Today I will show
You how grateful I am, not only by
the words that I speak,
but also by the way that I act.
Amen

Day 10

Going Along with the Crowd?

Obviously, I'm not trying to be a people pleaser!
No, I am trying to please God.

Galatians 1:10 NLT

If you're like most people, you have probably been tempted to "go along with the crowd" . . . even when the crowd was misbehaving. But here's something to think about: just because your friends may be misbehaving doesn't mean that you have to misbehave, too.

When people behave badly, they can spoil things in a hurry. So make sure that they don't spoil things for you.

So, if your friends misbehave, don't copy them! Instead, do the right thing. You'll be glad you did . . . and so will God!

You should forget about trying to be popular with everybody and start trying to be popular with God Almighty.

Sam Jones

A Parent's Tip!

Old-fashioned respect never goes out of fashion: Remember the good old days when parents demanded that their children be polite and respectful, especially to adults? For wise parents, those good old days are now.

A Kid's Tip!

You simply cannot please everybody. So here's what you should do: Try pleasing God and your parents.

Today's Prayer

Dear Lord, today I will honor You with
my thoughts, my actions, and my prayers.
I will try to please You,
and I will try to serve You.
Amen

Day 11

Obedience Is a Choice

Do what God's teaching says; when you only listen and do nothing, you are fooling yourselves.

James 1:22 NCV

You have a choice to make: are you going to be an obedient person or not? And remember: the decision to be obedient—or the decision not to be obedient—is a decision that you must make for yourself.

If you decide to behave yourself, you've made a smart choice. If you decide to obey your parents, you've made another smart choice. If you decide to pay attention to your teachers, you've made yet another wise choice. BUT . . . if you decide not to be obedient, you've made a silly choice.

What kind of person will you choose to be? An obedient, well-behaved person . . . or the opposite? Before you answer that question, here's something to think about: obedience pays . . . and disobedience doesn't.

Life is pretty much like a cafeteria line—
it offers us many choices, both good and bad.
Choose wisely.

Dennis Swanberg

A Parent's Tip!

Some things are not debatable: Some matters
should be strictly up to you, the parent. These kinds
of choices include issues of personal health and
safety and the core principles by which you, as a
concerned mom or dad, intend to raise your family.

A Kid's Tip!

When you make wise choices . . . You make
everybody happy. You make your parents happy, you
make your teachers happy, you make your friends
happy, and you make God happy!

Today's Prayer

Dear Lord, help me make choices that please You. Help me to be honest, patient, and kind. And above all, help me to follow the teachings of Jesus, not just today, but every day.
Amen

Day 12

If You're Not Sure What's Right, Ask Somebody!

Continue to ask, and God will give to you. Continue
to search, and you will find. Continue to knock,
and the door will open for you.

Matthew 7:7 ICB

When you're not sure about something, are you willing to ask your parents what you should do? Hopefully, when you have a question, you're not afraid to ask.

If you've got lots of questions, the Bible promises that God—like your parents—has answers, too.

So don't ever be afraid to ask questions. Both your parents and your Heavenly Father want to hear your questions . . . and they want to answer your questions as soon as you ask.

God guides through the counsel of good people.

E. Stanley Jones

A Parent's Tip!

Parents should ask for help, too. If you need something, ask. And remember this: God is listening, and He wants to hear from you right now.

A Kid's Tip!

Pray about it: Whatever it is, God can handle it. So ask Him to help you . . . and while you're at it, ask your parents for help, too.

Today's Prayer

Dear Lord, the Bible tells me that when
I ask for Your help, You will give it.
I thank You, Lord, for Your help,
for Your love, and for Your Son.
Amen

Day 13

Respecting Authority

Show respect for all people.
Love the brothers and sisters of God's family.

1 Peter 2:17 ICB

Are you polite and respectful to your parents and teachers? And do you do your best to treat everybody with the respect they deserve? If you want to obey God's rules, then you should be able to answer yes to these questions.

Remember this: the Bible teaches you to be a respectful person—and if it's right there in the Bible, it's certainly the right thing to do!

It is my calling to treat every human being with
grace and dignity, to treat every person,
whether encountered in a palace or a gas station,
as a life made in the image of God.

Sheila Walsh

A Parent's Tip!

Respect for authority starts with you. Remember
this: respect for those in authority begins at the
head of the household and works its way down from
there. And remember one more thing: your kids are
watching every move you make!

A Kid's Tip!

Everybody is a VIP: VIP means "Very Important
Person." To God, everybody is a VIP, and we should
treat every person with dignity, patience, and
respect.

Today's Prayer

Dear God, I pray for those who care
for me, especially my parents.
Give them wisdom, courage,
compassion, and faith.
Amen

Day 14

Learning How to Be Wise

Wisdom is a tree of life to those who embrace her;
happy are those who hold her tightly.

Proverbs 3:18 NLT

If you look in a dictionary, you'll see that the word "wisdom" means "using good judgement, and knowing what is true," But there's more: it's not enough just to know what's right; if you really want to become a wise person, you must also do what's right.

A big part of "doing what's right" is learning to be obedient . . . and the best time to start being a more obedient person is right now! Why? Because it's the wise thing to do.

Wisdom is knowledge applied.
Head knowledge is useless on the battlefield.
Knowledge stamped on the heart makes one wise.

Beth Moore

A Parent's Tip!

Parents make mistakes, too. When you are wrong, admit it. When you do, your children will learn that it's far better to fix problems than to ignore them.

A Kid's Tip!

When you are wrong, admit it. God will be happy and so will your parents.

Today's Prayer

Dear Lord, there's a right way to do things and a wrong way to do things. When I do things that are wrong, help me be quick to ask for forgiveness . . . and quick to correct my mistakes.
Amen

When You Don't Get Your Way
(Tantrums Are Not Us)

A foolish person loses his temper.
But a wise person controls his anger.

Proverbs 29:11 ICB

Temper tantrums are so silly. And so is pouting. So, of course, is whining. When we lose our tempers, we say things that we shouldn't say, and we do things that we shouldn't do. Too bad!

The Bible tells us that it is foolish to become angry and that it is wise to remain calm. That's why we should learn to control our tempers before our tempers control us.

Anger is a kind of temporary madness.

St. Basil the Great

A Parent's Tip!

Wise role models are a good thing to have: If you can control your anger, you'll help your children see the wisdom in controlling theirs.

A Kid's Tip!

No more temper tantrums! If you think you're about to throw a tantrum, slow down, catch your breath, and walk away if you must. It's better to walk away than it is to strike out in anger.

Today's Prayer

Dear Lord, help me to keep away from angry thoughts and angry people. And if I am tempted to have a temper tantrum, help me to calm down before I do.
Amen

Day 16

Making the Decision to Do What's Right

Keep your eyes focused on what is right.
Keep looking straight ahead to what is good.

Proverbs 4:25 ICB

Do you behave differently because you're a Christian? Or do you behave in pretty much the same way that you would if you had never heard of Jesus? Hopefully, your behavior is better because of the things you've learned from the Bible.

Doing the right thing is not always easy, especially when you're tired or frustrated. But, doing the wrong thing almost always leads to trouble. So here's some advice: remember the lessons you learn from the Bible. And keep remembering them every day of your life.

We need to be able to make decisions based on what we know rather than on what we feel.

Joyce Meyer

A Parent's Tip!

It's not just important to teach your child what to think. It's also important to teach your child how to think (and there's a big difference between the two).

A Kid's Tip!

Think ahead! Before you do something, ask yourself this question: "Will I be ashamed if my parents find out?" If the answer to that question is "Yes," don't do it!

Today's Prayer

Dear Lord, there's a right way
to do things and a wrong way.
Help me to do things the right way
today and every day.
Amen

Day 17

Pray About It!

Always be happy. Never stop praying.
Give thanks whatever happens.
That is what God wants for you in Christ Jesus.

1 Thessalonians: 5:16-18 ICB

Do you really want to become a more obedient person? Then pray about it. Would you like to learn how to behave yourself a little bit better? Then pray about it.

If you have questions about whether you should do something or not, pray about it. If there is something you're worried about, ask God to comfort you. And as you pray more, you'll discover that God is always near and that He's always ready to hear from you. So don't worry about things; pray about them. God is waiting . . . and listening!

Prayer accomplishes more than anything else.

Bill Bright

A Parent's Tip!

Don't ever be embarrassed to pray: Are you embarrassed to bow your head in a restaurant? Don't be; it's the people who aren't praying who should be embarrassed!

A Kid's Tip!

Eyelids closed . . . or not! When you are praying, the position of your eyelids makes little or no difference. Of course it's good to close your eyes and bow your head whenever you can, but it's also good to offer quick prayers to God with your eyes—and your heart—wide open.

Today's Prayer

Dear Lord, help me remember
the importance of prayer.
You always hear my prayers, God;
let me always pray them!
Amen

Choosing the Right Words

Don't use foul or abusive language.
Let everything you say be good and helpful,
so that your words will be an encouragement
to those who hear them.

Ephesians 4:29 NLT

Your words can help people . . . or not. Make certain that you're the kind of person who says helpful things, not hurtful things. You'll feel better about yourself when you help other people feel better about themselves.

Do you like for people to say kind words to you? Of course you do! And that's exactly how other people feel, too. That's why it's so important to say things that make people feel better, not worse.

Everybody needs to hear kind words, and that's exactly the kind of words they should hear from you!

When you talk, choose the very same words
that you would use if Jesus were looking over
your shoulder. Because He is.

Marie T. Freeman

A Parent's Tip!

Parents set the boundaries: Whether they realize it
or not, parents (not kids) establish the general tone
of the conversations that occur within their homes.
And it's up to parents to ensure that the tone of
those conversations is a tone that's pleasing to God.

A Kid's Tip!

Think before you speak: If you want to keep from
hurting other people's feelings, don't open your
mouth until you've turned on your brain.

Today's Prayer

Dear Lord, I will try to show respect to everybody, starting with my family and my friends. And, I will do my best to share the love that I feel in my heart for them . . . and for You!
Amen

Day 19

Sharing the Love

Jesus answered, "'Love the Lord your God with all
your heart, all your soul, and all your mind.'
This is the first and most important command.
And the second command is like the first:
'Love your neighbor as you love yourself.'
All the law and the writings of the prophets
depend on these two commands."

Matthew 22:37-40 NCV

The Bible teaches us that God is love and that if we wish to know Him, we must have love in our hearts. Sometimes, of course, when we're tired, angry, or frustrated, it is very hard for us to be loving. Thankfully, anger and frustration are feelings that come and go, but God's love lasts forever.

If you'd like to improve your day and your life, share God's love with your family and friends. Every time you love, and every time you give, God smiles.

The secret of a happy home life is
that the members of the family learn
to give and receive love.

Billy Graham

A Parent's Tip!

Be Expressive: Make certain that at your house,
love is expressed and demonstrated many times
each day. Little acts of consideration and kindness
can make a big difference in the way that your child
feels and the way your child behaves.

A Kid's Tip!

Express yourself . . . Since you love your family, you
should tell them so . . . a lot!

Today's Prayer

Dear Lord, today and every day,
I will tell my family that I love them.
And I will show my family that
I love them, too.
Amen

Day 20

Showing How We Love God

This is love for God: to obey his commands.

1 John 5:3 NIV

How can you show God how much you love Him? By obeying His commandments, that's how! When you follow God's rules, you show Him that you have real respect for Him and for His Son.

Sometimes, you will be tempted to disobey God, but don't do it. And sometimes you'll be tempted to disobey your parents or your teachers . . . but don't do that, either.

When your parent steps away or a teacher looks away, it's up to you to control yourself. And of this you can be sure: If you really want to control yourself, you can do it!

God's mark is on everything that obeys Him.

Martin Luther

A Parent's Tip!

Calling all parents! What the world needs is more parents who are willing to be positive role models to their children. God wants you to be that kind of parent . . . now!

A Kid's Tip!

When should you get tired of obeying God? The answer to that question is simple: Never!

Today's Prayer

Lord, let Your will be my will.
Let me always seek Your guidance
and Your will for my life.
Amen

Day 21

Obey Your Teachers

From a wise mind comes wise speech;
the words of the wise are persuasive.

Proverbs 16:23 NLT

It's good to obey your teachers, but before you can obey them, you must make sure you understand what your teachers are saying. So, in order to be an obedient student, you must be a student who knows how to listen.

Once you decide to be a careful listener, you'll become a better learner, too. But if you're determined to talk to other kids while your teachers are teaching, you won't learn very much.

So do yourself a favor: when you go to school, listen and obey. You'll be glad you did. . . and your teachers will be glad, too.

Obedience is the key of knowledge.

Christina Rossetti

A Parent's Tip!

Teaching the importance of teachers: You understand that your child's teachers are "Very Important People." Make certain that your child understands it, too.

A Kid's Tip!

Learning how to obey makes you a better person. You have many teachers. Listen to them and obey them. When you do, you'll become a better person.

Today's Prayer

Dear Lord, thank You for giving me
so many wise teachers. Help me listen
carefully to my teachers,
and help me learn from them.
Amen

Day 22

Good Deeds Are a Good Thing

A good person produces good deeds
from a good heart.

Luke 6:45 NLT

It's good to do good deeds. Even when nobody's watching, God is. And God knows whether you've done the right thing or the wrong thing.

So if you're tempted to misbehave when nobody is looking, remember this: There is never a time when "nobody's watching." Somebody is always watching over you—and that Somebody, of course, is your Father in heaven. Don't let Him down!

Seek to do good, and you will find that happiness
will run after you.

James Freeman Clarke

A Parent's Tip!

Parental love in action . . . Of course it's good to tell
your kids how you feel about them, but that's not
enough. You should also show your children how you
feel with your good deeds and your kind words.

A Kid's Tip!

You must do more than talk about it: In order to be
a good person, you must do good things. So get busy!
The best time to do a good deed is as soon as you
can do it!

Today's Prayer

Dear Lord, let me help others like
Jesus did. I will serve them with
my good deeds and with my prayers,
and I will give thanks for all those
who serve and protect our nation
and our world.
Amen

Day 23

It's Always the Right Time to Praise God

Happy are the people who know how to praise you.
Lord, let them live in the light of your presence.

Psalm 89:15 NCV

If you're like most kids, you're very busy doing things and learning things. But no matter how busy you are—even if you hardly have a moment to spare—you should still slow down and say "Thank You," to God (And remember: a great way to thank God is to obey Him!).

God has given you many things, and you owe Him everything, including a GREAT BIG THANK YOU, starting now (and ending never!).

Praise Him! Praise Him!
Tell of His excellent greatness.
Praise Him! Praise Him!
Ever in joyful song!

Fanny Crosby

A Parent's Tip!

If you need a little cheering up, start counting your blessings . . . and keep counting until you feel better.

A Kid's Tip!

One of the reasons you go to church is to praise God. But, you need not wait until Sunday rolls around to thank your Heavenly Father. Instead, you can praise Him many times each day by saying silent prayers that only He can hear.

Today's Prayer

Dear Lord, today I will thank You for all
Your blessings. And I'll do the same thing
tomorrow, and every day after that.
You never stop loving me,
and I will never stop praising You.
Amen

Day 24

What Kind of Example?

You are the light that gives light to the world . . .
Live so that they will see the good things you do.
Live so that they will praise your Father in heaven.

Matthew 5:14, 16 ICB

What kind of example are you? Are you the kind of person who shows other people what it means to be obedient and kind? Hopefully so!!!

Are you willing to obey your parents? And are you willing to obey God? If so, then you're bound to be a good example to other people. And that's a good thing because God needs people like you who are willing to stand up and be counted for Him.

More depends on my walk than my talk.

D. L. Moody

A Parent's Tip!

Words are never enough: When it comes to teaching our children the most important lessons, the things we say pale in comparison to the things we do. Being a responsible parent is a big job, but don't fret: you and God, working together, can handle it!

A Kid's Tip!

Let your light shine . . . The way that you behave yourself is like a light that shines out upon the world. Make sure that your light is both bright and good.

Today's Prayer

Dear Lord, make me a good example to
my family and friends. Let the things
that I say and do show everybody
what it means to be a good person
and a good Christian.

Amen

Day 25

Obey and Be Joyful

Light shines on the godly, and joy on those who
do right. May all who are godly be happy
in the Lord and praise his holy name.

Psalm 97:11-12 NLT

A man named C. S. Lewis once said, "Joy is the serious business of heaven." And he was right! God seriously wants you to be a seriously joyful person.

One way that you can have a more joyful life is by learning how to become a more obedient person. When you do, you'll stay out of trouble, and you'll have lots more time for fun.

So here's a way to be a more joyful, happy person: do the right thing! It's the best way to live.

Joy is the echo of God's life within us.

Joseph Marmion

A Parent's Tip!

Joy is contagious: Remember that a joyful family starts with joyful parents.

A Kid's Tip!

Joy doesn't come from having things . . . Joy comes from doing the right thing.

Today's Prayer

Dear Lord, I want to be a joyful Christian, and I know that my joy depends, in part, on my obedience. Today, I will try to be both obedient and joyful.

Amen

Day 26

Choosing Your Friends

A friend loves you all the time.

Proverbs 17:17 ICB

Are your friends the kind of kids who encourage you to behave yourself? If so, you've chosen your friends wisely.

But if your friends try to get you in trouble, perhaps it's time to think long and hard about making some new friends.

Whether you know it or not, you're probably going to behave like your friends behave. So pick out friends who make you want to behave better, not worse. When you do, you'll be saving yourself from a lot of trouble . . . a whole lot of trouble.

Do you want to be wise? Choose wise friends.

Charles Swindoll

A Parent's Tip!

Help from the sidelines: As parents, we can't make friendships for our children, but we can coach them on the art of making friends. All of us, whether youngsters or grown-ups, make friends by treating others as we wish to be treated.

A Kid's Tip!

You make friends by being a friend. And when you choose your friends, choose wisely.

Today's Prayer

Thank You, Lord, for the Friend
I have in Jesus. And, thank You for
all my other friends, too.
Amen

Saying
What's Right

Speak the truth to each other . . . .

Zechariah 8:16 NIV

Sometimes, it's hard to know exactly what to say. And sometimes, it can be very tempting to say something that isn't true—or something that isn't nice. But when you say things you shouldn't say, you'll regret it later.

So make this promise to yourself, and keep it—promise to think about the things you say before you say them. And whatever you do, always tell the truth. When you do these things, you'll be doing yourself a big favor, and you'll be obeying the Word of God.

Those who walk in truth walk in liberty.

Beth Moore

A Parent's Tip!

Words, words, words . . . are important, important, important! And, some of the most important words you will ever speak are the ones that your children hear. So whether or not you are talking directly to your kids, choose your words carefully.

A Kid's Tip!

If you're not sure that it's the right thing to say, don't say it! And if you're not sure that it's the truth, don't tell it.

Today's Prayer

Dear Lord, when I'm about to say
something, help me think about
my words before I say them, not after.
Amen

Day 28

Jesus Is
Our Example

I have set you an example that you should do
as I have done for you.

John 13:15 NIV

How do people know that you're a Christian? Well, you can tell them, of course. And make no mistake about it: talking about your faith in God is a very good thing to do. But telling people about Jesus isn't enough. You should also show people how a Christian (like you) should behave.

God wants you to be loving and giving. That way, when another person sees how you behave, that person will know what it means to be a good Christian . . . a good Christian like you!

In his life, Christ is an example showing us
how to live.

Martin Luther

A Parent's Tip!

Kids imitate their parents, so act accordingly! The
best way for your children to learn how to follow
in Christ's footsteps is by following you while you
follow Him!

A Kid's Tip!

If you want to be a little more like Christ . . . learn
about His teachings, follow in His footsteps, and
obey His commandments.

Today's Prayer

Dear Lord, You sent Jesus to save
the world and to save me. I thank You
for Jesus, and I will do my best to
follow Him, today and forever.
Amen

Day 29

Patience Pays

Always be humble and gentle.
Be patient and accept each other with love.

Ephesians 4:2 ICB

The dictionary defines the word "patience" as the ability to be calm, tolerant, and understanding. Here's what that means: the word "calm" means being in control of your emotions (not letting your emotions control you). The word "tolerant" means being kind and considerate to people who are different from you. And, the word "understanding" means being able to put yourself in another person's shoes.

If you can be calm, tolerant, and understanding, you will be the kind of person whose good deeds are a blessing to your family and friends. And that's exactly the kind of person that God wants you to be.

If only we could be as patient with other people
as God is with us!

Jim Gallery

A Parent's Tip!

Kids imitate their parents, so act accordingly! The
best way for your child to learn to be patient is by
example . . . your example!

A Kid's Tip!

Be patient, and follow the rules . . . even if you
don't like some of the rules that you're supposed to
follow, follow them anyway.

Today's Prayer

Lord, sometimes it's hard to be a patient
person, and that's exactly when I should
try my hardest to be patient.
Help me to obey Your commandments
by being a patient, loving Christian,
even when it's hard.
Amen

Day 30

The Golden Rule

Do for other people the same things
you want them to do for you.

Matthew 7:12 ICB

How should you treat other people? Jesus has the answer to that question. Jesus wants you to treat other people exactly like you want to be treated: with kindness, respect, and courtesy. When you do, you'll make your family and friends happy . . . and that's what God wants.

So if you're wondering how to treat someone else, follow the Golden Rule: treat the other people like you want them to treat you. When you do, you'll be obeying your Father in heaven and you'll be making other folks happy at the same time.

The #1 rule of friendship is the Golden one.

Marie T. Freeman

A Parent's Tip!

The Golden Rule . . . is as good as gold—in fact, it's better than gold. And as a responsible parent, you should make certain that your child knows that the Golden Rule is, indeed, golden.

A Kid's Tip!

How would you feel? When you're trying to decide how to treat another person, ask yourself this question: "How would I feel if somebody treated me that way?" Then, treat the other person the way that you would want to be treated.

Today's Prayer

Dear God, help me remember to treat
other people in the same way that
I would want to be treated if I were in
their shoes. The Golden Rule is Your rule,
Father; I'll make it my rule, too.

Amen

Day 31

The Right Kind of Attitude

Your attitude should be the same that
Christ Jesus had.

Philippians 2:5 NLT

What does the word "attitude" mean? "Attitude" means "the way that you think." And your attitude is important. Your attitude can make you happy or sad, grumpy or glad, joyful or mad. Your attitude doesn't just control the way that you think; it also controls how you behave. If you have a good attitude, you'll behave yourself. And if you have a bad attitude, you're more likely to misbehave.

You have more control over your attitude than you think. One way you can improve your attitude is by learning about Jesus and about His attitude toward life. When you do, you'll learn that it's always better to think good thoughts, and it's always better to do good things. Always!

Keep on smiling and the whole world smiles with you.

Dennis Swanberg

A Parent's Tip!

Kids are very intuitive: Believe it or not, your child is probably a mind reader. If your kid is like most kids, he or she is surprisingly sensitive. So do yourself and your child a favor: be careful with your thoughts as well as your actions.

A Kid's Tip!

You can choose to have a good attitude or a not-so-good attitude. And it's a choice you make every day.

Today's Prayer

Dear Lord, I pray for an attitude that pleases You. Even when I'm angry, unhappy, tired, or upset, I pray that I can remember what it means to be a good person and a good Christian.
Amen

Day 32

If You Make a Mistake

For all have sinned and fall short of
the glory of God.

Romans 3:23 HCSB

Do you make mistakes? Of course you do . . . everybody does.

When you make a mistake, what's your attitude about it? Do you apologize to the people you've hurt, and do you try to fix things as soon as possible. And do you try to learn from your mistakes? Hopefully so.

When you make a mistake, you must try to learn from it so that you won't make the very same mistake again. And, if you have hurt someone—or if you have disobeyed God—you must ask for forgiveness.

Remember: mistakes are a part of life, but the biggest mistake you can make is to keep making the same mistake over and over and over again.

God is able to take mistakes, when they are committed to Him, and make of them something for our good and for His glory.

Ruth Bell Graham

A Parent's Tip!

The perfect parent does not exist. So don't be too hard on yourself when you fall short of absolute perfection. Do your best, and trust God with the rest.

A Kid's Tip!

Made a mistake? Ask for forgiveness? If you've broken one of God's rules, you can always ask Him for His forgiveness. And He will always give it!

Today's Prayer

Dear Lord, thank You for loving me, even when I make mistakes. You forgive me, Lord, and so do my parents. Let me learn to forgive others, so that I can treat other people in the very same way that I have been treated.

Amen

Day 33

Learn to Control Yourself

So prepare your minds for service and have self-control. All your hope should be for the gift of grace that will be yours when Jesus Christ is shown to you.

1 Peter 1:13 NCV

Are you learning how to control yourself? If the answer to that question is yes, then you deserve a big cheer because God wants all His children (including you) to behave themselves.

Sometimes, it's hard to be a well-behaved person, especially if you have friends who don't behave nicely. But if your friends misbehave, don't imitate them. Instead, listen to your conscience, talk to your parents, and do the right thing . . . NOW!

Man's great danger is the combination of
his increased control over the elements
and his lack of control over himself.

Albert Schweitzer

A Parent's Tip!

If you expect your child to have self-control, then
you must have it, too. When it comes to parenting,
you can't really teach it if you won't really live it.

A Kid's Tip!

Think first! Think before you say things . . . and
think before you do things. Otherwise, you can
get yourself into trouble. So here's a good rule to
follow: Slow down long enough to think about the
things you're about to do or say. That way, you'll
make better choices.

Today's Prayer

Dear God, today I will slow down and think about things before I do them. And when I slow down to think about things, I will always try to do what's right.

Amen

Obedience Pleases God

Therefore, whether we are at home or away,
we make it our aim to be pleasing to Him.

2 Corinthians 5:9 HCSB

re you interested in pleasing God? Are you interested in pleasing your parents? And your teachers? If so, try your best to be obedient. When you try hard to do the right thing, you'll make other people feel better—and you'll make yourself feel better, too.

God knows everything about you. And when you do what's right, God is pleased . . . very pleased.

God is not hard to please. He does not expect us to be absolutely perfect. He just expects us to keep moving toward Him and believing in Him, letting Him work with us to bring us into conformity to His will and ways.

Joyce Meyer

A Parent's Tip!

Parental attitudes are contagious. It's up to you to live your life—and treat your family—in a way that pleases God because He's watching carefully . . . and so, for that matter, are your kids.

A Kid's Tip!

How can you please God? By having a good attitude, by obeying your parents and your teachers, and being kind to your friends.

Today's Prayer

Dear Lord, thank You for all
the blessings You have given me.
Today and every day I will do my best
to please You by thinking good thoughts
and doing good deeds.
Amen

Day 35

It Starts in the Heart

We must be sure to obey the truth
we have learned already.

Philippians 3:16 NLT

An attitude of obedience starts in your heart and works its way out from there.

Do you listen to your heart when it tells you to behave yourself? Hopefully, you do. After all, you'll be happier and healthier when you do the right thing.

So don't forget to listen to your parents. And while you're at it, don't forget to listen to your conscience. When you listen carefully, you'll be obedient . . . and you'll make everybody glad, including yourself!

You may not always see immediate results,
but all God wants is your obedience
and faithfulness.

Vonette Bright

A Parent's Tip!

Obedience Begins at Home. If your children don't
learn obedience between the four walls of your
home, they probably won't learn it anywhere else.

A Kid's Tip!

When you obey your parents . . . you're pleasing
God, you're pleasing your parents, and you're doing
yourself a BIG favor.

Today's Prayer

Dear Lord, help me remember
the importance of prayer.
You always hear my prayers, God;
let me always pray them!
Amen

Day 36

Honesty Is the Best Policy

Doing what is right brings freedom to honest people.

Proverbs 11:6 ICB

Have you ever said something that wasn't true? When you did, were you sorry for what you had said? Probably so.

When we're dishonest, we make ourselves unhappy in surprising ways. Here are just a few troubles that result from dishonesty: we feel guilty and we are usually found out and we disappoint others and we disappoint God. It's easy to see that lies always cause more problems than they solve.

Happiness and honesty always go hand in hand. But it's up to you to make sure that you go hand in hand with them!

I hold the maxim no less applicable to public
than to private affairs,
that honesty is the best policy.

George Washington

A Parent's Tip!

The truth can be hard for parents, too: telling the truth isn't just hard for kids. And when honesty is hard, that's precisely the moment when wise parents remember that their children are watching . . . and learning.

A Kid's Tip!

When telling the truth is hard . . . it probably means that you're afraid of what others might think—or what they might do—if you're truthful. But even when telling the truth is hard, it's always the right thing to do.

Today's Prayer

Dear Lord, sometimes it's hard to tell the truth. But even when telling the truth is difficult, let me follow Your commandment. Honesty isn't just the best policy, Lord; it's Your policy, and I will obey You by making it my policy, too.

Amen

Day 37

Slow Down and Listen

Wise people can also listen and learn.

Proverbs 1:5 NCV

When God made you, He gave you two ears and one mouth for a very good reason: you can learn at least twice as much by listening as you can by talking. That's why it's usually better to listen first and talk second. But when you're frustrated or tired, it's easy to speak first and think later.

A big part of growing up is learning how to slow down long enough to listen to the things that people have to say. So the next time you're tempted to turn off your ears and tune up your mouth, stop, listen, and think. After all, God gave you two wonderful ears for a very good reason: to use them.

Listening is loving.

Zig Ziglar

A Parent's Tip!

Great communicators listen first and speak second; poor communicators complete the same tasks, but in reverse order.

A Kid's Tip!

Listening Shows You Care: When you listen to the things other people have to say, it shows that you care about their message and about them. Listening carefully is not just the courteous thing to do, it's also the kind thing to do.

Today's Prayer

Dear Lord, I have lots to learn.
Help me to watch, to listen, to think,
and to learn, every day of my life.
Amen

Day 38

Knowing Right from Wrong . . . and Doing It!

Praise the Lord! Happy are those who respect
the Lord, who want what he commands.

Psalm 112:1 NCV

Since you're old enough to know right from wrong, you're old enough to do something about it. In other words, you should always try to do the right thing, and you should also do your very best not to do the wrong thing.

When you learn to obey your parents and teachers, the easier it is to do the right thing. And when you learn to think first and do things next, you avoid lots of silly mistakes. So here's great advice: first, slow down long enough to figure out the right thing to do—and then do it. You'll make yourself happy, and you'll make lots of other people happy, too.

If we have the true love of God in our hearts,
we will show it in our lives. We will not have to go
up and down the earth proclaiming it.
We will show it in everything we say or do.

D. L. Moody

A Parent's Tip!

Obedience begins at home. If your children don't learn obedience between the four walls of your home, they probably won't learn it anywhere else.

A Kid's Tip!

When in doubt, ask mom or dad: If you're not sure whether or not something is right or wrong, ask your parents before you do it!

Today's Prayer

Dear Lord, when I'm tempted to do the wrong thing, help me to slow down and to think about my behavior. And then, help me to know what's right and to do what's right.

Amen

Day 39

Going to Church

Let's see how inventive we can be in encouraging love
and helping out, not avoiding worshipping together
as some do but spurring each other on.

Hebrews 10:24-25 MSG

When your parents take you to church, are you pleased to go? Hopefully so. After all, church is a wonderful place to learn about God's rules.

The church belongs to God just as surely as you belong to God. That's why the church is a good place to learn about God and about His Son Jesus.

So when your mom and dad take you to church, remember this: church is a fine place to be . . . and you're lucky to be there.

The church is where it's at.
The first place of Christian service for any Christian
is in a local church.

Jerry Clower

A Parent's Tip!

Make church a celebration, not an obligation: Your
attitude towards church will help determine your
kid's attitude toward church . . . so celebrate
accordingly!

A Kid's Tip!

Forget the Excuses: If somebody starts making up
reasons not to go to church, don't pay any attention
. . . even if that person is you!

Today's Prayer

Dear Lord, thank You for Your church.
I'll go to church and support it.
I'll help build Your church, Lord,
in every way I can.
Amen

Day 40

Self-control

Knowing God leads to self-control.
Self-control leads to patient endurance,
and patient endurance leads to godliness.

2 Peter 1:6 NLT

Learning how to control yourself helps you become a more obedient person. So the more you learn about self-control, the better.

Learning how to control yourself is a good thing. Self-control helps you at home, at school, and at church. That's why parents and teachers are happy to talk about the rewards of good behavior.

If you want to learn more about self-control, ask your parents. They'll help you figure out better ways to behave yourself. And that's good for everybody . . . especially you!

Your thoughts are the determining factor
as to whose mold you are conformed to.
Control your thoughts and you control
the direction of your life.

Charles Stanley

A Parent's Tip!

Self-control at school starts at home: teachers can
certainly help, but we cannot expect them to re-
train our children. When it comes to the importance
of self-control, we, as parents, must be the ones to
teach our kids how to behave.

A Kid's Tip!

A big part of growing up . . . is learning how to
control yourself.

Today's Prayer

Dear Lord, I want to be able to control myself better and better each day. Help me find better ways to behave myself, ways that are pleasing to You.
Amen

Day 41

Show Respect
for Others

Show respect for all people:
Love the brothers and sisters of God's family.
1 Peter 2:17 NCV

Do you try to have a respectful attitude towards everybody? Hopefully so!

Should you be respectful of grown ups? Of course. Teachers? Certainly. Family members? Yes. Friends? Yep, but it doesn't stop there. The Bible teaches us to treat all people with respect.

Respect for others is habit-forming: the more you do it, the easier it becomes. So start practicing right now. Say lots of kind words and do lots of kind things, because when it comes to kindness and respect, practice makes perfect.

It is my calling to treat every human being with grace and dignity, to treat every person, whether encountered in a palace or a gas station, as a life made in the image of God.

Sheila Walsh

A Parent's Tip!

Children may seek to find humor in the misfortunes of others; children may, on occasion, exhibit cruelty towards other children. Be watchful for such behaviors and correct them with enthusiasm and vigor.

A Kid's Tip!

VIP means "Very Important Person," and to God, everybody is a VIP. That means you should treat every person with dignity, patience, and respect.

Today's Prayer

Dear Lord, let me remember to be
respectful and kind to everybody,
starting with my family and friends.
And, let me share the love that I feel in
my heart with them . . . and with You!
Amen

Day 42

When You Need to Be Forgiven

You know the Lord is full of mercy and is kind.

James 5:11 NCV

When you do something you shouldn't have done, here are some things you can do:

1. Apologize to the people you've hurt, and ask for their forgiveness;
2. Fix the things you've messed up or broken;
3. Don't make the same mistake again;
4. Ask God for His forgiveness (which, by the way, He will give to you instantly);
5. Get busy doing something you can be proud of.
6. Don't be too hard on yourself . . . even if you made a mistake, you're still a very, very special person!

Forgiveness is rarely easy, but it is always right.

Cynthia Heald

A Parent's Tip!

Granting forgiveness can be hard. No matter. God instructs us to forgive others (and to keep forgiving them), period. As a parent, you must explain to your child that forgiving another person—even when it's difficult—is the right thing to do.

A Kid's Tip!

If you're having trouble forgiving someone else . . . think how many times other people have forgiven you!

Today's Prayer

Dear Lord, I have made mistakes, and You have forgiven me. Thank You for Your forgiveness. When I am not perfect, help other people to forgive me—and help me forgive myself.

Amen

Day 43

Be Kind!

A kind person is doing himself a favor.
But a cruel person brings trouble upon himself.

Proverbs 11:17 ICB

Sometimes, young people can be very mean. They may make fun of other people, and when they do so, it's wrong. Period.

As Christians, we should be kind to everyone. And, if other kids say unkind things to a child or make fun of him or her, it's up to us to step in and lend a helping hand.

Today and every day, be a person who is known for your kindness, not for your cruelty. That's how God wants you to behave. Period.

Showing kindness to others is one of
the nicest things we can do for ourselves.

Janette Oke

A Parent's Tip!

Play fair. Never try to win an argument by hurting
another person; it's simply not worth it. Besides,
your kids are probably watching.

A Kid's Tip!

Don't be cruel: Sometimes, you can be too honest,
especially if you say unkind things that are intended
to hurt other people's feelings. When you're
deciding what to say, you should mix honesty and
courtesy together. When you do, you'll say the right
thing.

Today's Prayer

Dear Lord, sometimes people are cruel.
Let me never be such a person.
Let me treat others as I wish to be
treated, and let my thoughts and actions
honor You today and forever.
Amen

Day 44

Keep Counting Your Blessings!

Enter his gates with thanksgiving,
go into his courts with praise.
Give thanks to him and bless his name.

Psalm 100:4 NLT

How long would it take to count all your blessings? A very, very long time! Your blessings include your life, your family, your friends, your talents, and your possessions, for starters. But, your greatest blessing—a gift that is yours for the asking—is God's gift of eternal life through Christ Jesus.

You can never count up every single blessing that God has given you, but it doesn't hurt to try . . . so get ready, get set, go—start counting your blessings RIGHT NOW!

Jesus intended for us to be overwhelmed by the blessings of regular days. He said it was the reason he had come: "I am come that they might have life, and that they might have it more abundantly."

Gloria Gaither

A Parent's Tip!

Be imaginative: There are so many ways to say, "I love you." Find them. Put love notes in lunch pails and on pillows; hug relentlessly; laugh, play, and pray without abandon. Remember that love is highly contagious, and that your task, as a parent, is to ensure that your children catch it.

A Kid's Tip!

Make your feelings known to God. Of course you are thankful to God for all His blessings, starting, of course, with your family and your friends. Tell Him so.

Today's Prayer

Dear Lord, today I will begin counting
my blessings . . . and I will keep counting
them every day of my life.
Amen

Day 45

Stop, Look, and Think!

A wise person is patient.

Proverbs 19:11 ICB

The Book of Proverbs tells us that self-control and patience are very good things to have. But for most of us, self-control and patience can also be very hard things to learn.

Are you having trouble being patient? And are you having trouble slowing down long enough to think before you act? If so, remember that self-control takes practice, and lots of it, so keep trying. And if you make a mistake, don't be too upset. After all, if you're going to be a really patient person, you shouldn't just be patient with others; you should also be patient with yourself.

If you don't look before you leap,
you may start having regrets even before you land.

Jim Gallery

A Parent's Tip!

It's always a good time to put the brakes on impulsive behavior . . . theirs and yours!

A Kid's Tip!

Stop, think, then speak: If you want to make your words useful instead of hurtful, don't open your mouth until you've turned on your brain!

Today's Prayer

Dear Lord, let me be patient with other people's mistakes. And let me be patient with my own. I know that I still have so many things to learn. I won't stop learning, I won't give up, and I won't stop growing up. Every day, I will do my best to become a little bit more like the person You intend for me to be.

Amen

Day 46

Your Parents Are Smarter Than You Think

My child, listen to your father's teaching.
And do not forget your mother's advice.
Proverbs 1:8 ICB

Do you listen carefully to the things your parents tell you? You should. Your parents want the very best for you. They want you to be happy and healthy; they want you to be smart and to do smart things. Your parents have much to teach you, and you have much to learn. So listen carefully to the things your mom and dad have to say. And ask lots of questions. When you do, you'll soon discover that your parents have lots of answers . . . lots of very good answers.

The home should be a school where
life's basic lessons are taught.

Billy Graham

A Parent's Tip!

Have a few important rules . . . and enforce them:
No matter how big your children are, they still need
to abide by your rules if they want to reside under
your roof.

A Kid's Tip!

Talking Versus Really Talking: Don't be too
embarrassed or too fearful to tell your parents
what you're really thinking about. They understand
more than you think they do!

Today's Prayer

Lord, let me be respectful of all people,
starting with my family and friends.
And, let me share the love that I feel
in my heart with them . . . and with You!
Amen

Day 47

Watch What You Think

Fix your thoughts on what is true and honorable
and right. Think about things that are pure
and lovely and admirable. Think about things
that are excellent and worthy of praise.

Philippians 4:8 NLT

Do you try to think the kind of thoughts that make you happy, not sad? The Bible says that you should.

Do you try to think about things that are true and right? The Bible says that you should.

Do you turn away from bad thoughts—and away from people who misbehave? The Bible says that you should.

The Bible instructs you to guard your thoughts against things that are hurtful or wrong. So remember this: when you turn away from the bad thoughts and bad people, you've made a very wise choice.

It is the thoughts and intents of the heart
that shape a person's life.

John Eldredge

A Parent's Tip!

If your thoughts tend toward the negative end of
the spectrum, redirect them. How? You can start by
counting your blessings and by thanking your Father
in heaven. And while you're at it, train yourself to
begin thinking thoughts that are more rational, more
accepting, and more upbeat . . . for everybody's
sake.

A Kid's Tip!

Good thoughts lead to good deeds and bad thoughts
lead elsewhere. So guard your thoughts accordingly.

Today's Prayer

Dear Lord, help me think about things
that are good, things that are true,
and things that are right . . .
starting right now!
Amen

You Don't Have to Go Along with the Crowd

Do you think I am trying to make people accept me?
No, God is the One I am trying to please.
Am I trying to please people? If I still wanted to
please people, I would not be a servant of Christ.

Galatians 1:10 NCV

It happens to all of us at one time or another: a friend asks us to do something that we think is wrong. What should we do? Should we try to please our friend by doing something bad? No way! It's not worth it!

Trying to please our friends is okay. What's not okay is misbehaving in order to do so.

Do you have a friend who encourages you to misbehave? Hopefully you don't have any friends like that. But if you do, say "No, NO, NOOOOOO!" And what if your friend threatens to break up the friendship? Let him! Friendships like that just aren't worth it.

Those who follow the crowd usually get lost in it.

Rick Warren

A Parent's Tip!

Be a good example: If you are burdened with a "people-pleasing" personality, outgrow it. Realize that you can't please all of the people all of the time (including your children), nor should you attempt to.

A Kid's Tip!

Face facts: since you can't please everybody, you're better off trying to please the people who are trying to help you become a better person, not the people who are encouraging you to misbehave!

Today's Prayer

Dear Lord, there's a right way
and a wrong way to do things. Let me do
what's right and keep doing what's
right every day of my life.
Amen

Day 49

Following Directions

In all your ways acknowledge Him,
and He shall direct your paths.

Proverbs 3:6 NKJV

Directions, directions, directions. It seems like somebody is always giving you directions: telling you where to go, how to behave, and what to do next. But sometimes all these directions can be confusing! How can you understand everything that everybody tells you? The answer, of course, is that you must pay careful attention to those directions . . . and that means listening.

To become a careful listener, here are some things you must do:

1. Don't talk when you're supposed to be listening (your ears work best when your mouth is closed);
2. Watch the person who's giving the directions (when your eyes and ears work together, it's easier to understand things);
3. If you don't understand something, ask a question (it's better to ask now than to make a mistake later).

Obedience is the outward expression
of your love of God.

Henry Blackaby

A Parent's Tip!

You don't have to haul your kid to a deserted island
to have a meaningful conversation. Meaningful moments between you and your child can happen anywhere—and it's up to you to make sure that they do.

A Kid's Tip!

If you're afraid to raise your hand and ask a
question, remember this . . . if you don't understand
something, lots of other people in the classroom
probably don't understand it, either. So you'll be
doing everybody a big favor if you raise your hand
and ask your question.

Today's Prayer

Dear Lord, let me listen carefully to my parents, to my teachers, and to You. When I listen, I learn. Let me become a better listener today than I was yesterday, and let me become an even better listener tomorrow.

Amen

Day 50

For God So Loved the World

For God so loved the world that he gave
his only Son, so that everyone who believes in him
will not perish but have eternal life.

John 3:16 NLT

How much does God love you? He loves you so much that He sent His Son Jesus to come to this earth for you! And, when you accept Jesus into your heart, God gives you a gift that is more precious than gold: that gift is called "eternal life" which means that you will live forever with God in heaven!

God's love is bigger and more powerful than anybody can imagine, but it is very real. So do yourself a favor right now: accept God's love with open arms and welcome His Son Jesus into your heart. When you do, your life will be changed today, tomorrow, and forever.

The greatest love of all is God's love for us,
a love that showed itself in action.

Billy Graham

A Parent's Tip!

The kids are watching . . . Children form their ideas
about God's love by experiencing their parents' love.
Live—and love—accordingly.

A Kid's Tip!

God's love is your greatest security blanket. Think
how much your parents love you and then know that
God loves you even more.

Today's Prayer

Dear God, the Bible teaches me that
Your love lasts forever. Thank You, God,
for Your love. Let me trust
Your promises, and let me live
according to Your teachings,
not just for today, but forever.
Amen